This book is dedicated to children of all ages who have discovered and who will discover that their eyes are their keys to drawing. I wish them the joy of seeing and the pleasure of recording the things they see and the ideas they imagine. I wish them the confidence in drawing that is their birthright.

Jean Morman Unsworth

Thanks to the teachers who piloted the lessons in *Drawing Is Basic* and who sent in their students' drawings.

Lin Ferrell
Visual Arts Instructional Specialist
Chesterfield County Public Schools
Richmond, Virginia, and the
art teachers of Chesterfield County

Teri Power, art specialist
School District of
New Richmond, Wisconsin

Eva Dubowski, art teacher
Infant of Prague School
Flossmoor, Illinois

Andrea Rowe, classroom teacher
St. Damian School
Oak Forest, Illinois

Catherine Kestler, art teacher,
and classroom teachers of
Sacred Heart Academy
Chicago, Illinois

Barbara Perez, art teacher
St. Athanasius School
Evanston, Illinois

Dorothy Johnson, art supervisor
Volusia County Schools
Florida

Wanda Baer, art teacher
Mount Carmel Academy
Chicago, Illinois

Additional thanks to the classroom teachers in the following Chicago, Illinois schools: St. Matthias School, Children of Peace School, and St. Gertrude School.

A special thank you to all the young artists who performed the drawing exercises in this book and whose drawings add a unique charm to *Drawing Is Basic*.

Duong Nguyen

Garrett Ducas

Adam Wiessert

Maureen Gallagher

Katie Rose DeCillo

Jackie Dal Santo

Tim Curran

Katie Curtis

Colleen Vande Hey

Tom Robbins

Johnathan Tucker

Herbert Garcia

LeRoy Pinto

Lizzy Robbins

Margaret Burke

Alexandra Hayden

Fred Hunt

Heather Williams

Sarah Hults

John Harrison

Brittany Toth

Courtney Miles

Emmett Byrne

Ben Limpinyabul

Elizabeth Ospina

Maga Sacco

Arthur Pethukov

Marike Monis

Edson Juarez

Evan Davis

Brian Burns

Demi Giannaras

Israel Neumann

Jill Mettler

Trent O'Connor

John Neuman

Becky Martinez

Kevin Donohue

Ashley McKay

Ed Graft

Elizabeth Moeykens

Anthony Ferris

Chris Conroy

Karoline Roderer

Neal H. McCarthy

Elizabeth McCullough

Natalie Callaghan

Dahn Vinh Cran

Jonathan Curran

Michelle Petty

Kristen Zeiler

Dillon O'Neill

Erica Torvick

Kevin Mitchell

Albert Starshak

Philip Syversten

Ryan Hoesley

Molly Boyd

Lauren Kessler

Abby Crick

Anne Karlovitz

Nick Gauna

Lily Amberg

Trish Keppler

Jennifer Stanley

Tori Hughes

Javonne Patrick

Willie Mosley

Heather Nichols

Emily Humerickhouse

Sarah Fagan

Jessica Chan

Atiya Husain

Janelle Lewis

Leana Garcia

Delaney Davoie

Josh Kinder

Kenneth DeHaan

Erin Fenn

Alicia Thomas

Morgan Hanley

Adam Weissert

Anna Williams

Becky Martinez

Natalia Salazar

Danielle Kindler

Rokas Darulis

June Kendall

Will Shotwell

Thomas Woodley

Addison Cihlar

Glenita R.

GRADE 6

Drawing is a basic way of seeing and expressing. Every child can draw, but too many children are daunted by the fear that what they draw will not look "right." It is your joyous opportunity to encourage each of your students to draw and write with comfort and confidence.

Jean Morman Unsworth

DALE SEYMOUR PUBLICATIONS®

Parsippany, New Jersey

Editorial Manager: Carolyn Coyle
Senior Editor: Mary Ellen Gilbert
Production/Manufacturing Director: Janet Yearian
Production/Manufacturing Manager: Karen Edmonds
Production/Manufacturing Coordinator: Lorraine Allen
Art Director: Jim O'Shea
Text and Cover Design: Robert Dobaczewski

Credits

Chagall, Marc (1887–1985), *An der Staffelei (At the Easel),* 1922, dry point.

Kollwitz, Kathe, (1867–1945), *Self Portrait,* lithograph. Courtesy of R. S. Johnson International Gallery, Chicago, IL.

Unsworth, Jean Morman, *Tiger Lily,* pencil, p. 28; *Artist's Point, Yellowstone National Park, Colorado,* pencil, p. 31; *Sketch of Cave Painting, Lascaux, France,* pencil, p. 64; *Birds on a Wire,* ink line, p. 66; *Badlands, South Dakota,* pencil, p. 79; *Moltrasio, Lake Como, Italy,* pen and charcoal, p. 80; *Williamsburg House,* photograph, p. 92.

Dale Seymour Publications
An imprint of Pearson Learning
299 Jefferson Road, P.O. Box 480
Parsippany, New Jersey 07054-0480

www.pearsonlearning.com

1-800-321-3106

Dale Seymour Publications® is a registered trademark of Dale Seymour Publications, Inc.

ISBN 0-7690-2502-1

1 2 3 4 5 6 7 8 9 10-ML-04 03 02 01 00

This Book Is Printed
On Recycled Paper

Contents

1. Daily Exercises in
   Perception

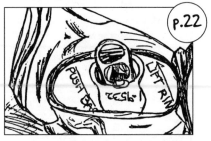

p.22

2. Drawing in 3-D

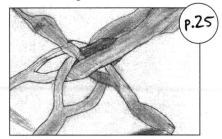

p.25

3. Connecting to All
   of Your Senses

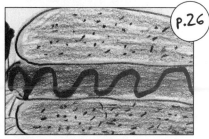

p.26

4. Drawing Flowers

p.27

5. Drawing Trees

p.29

6. Drawing Textures

p.32

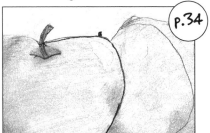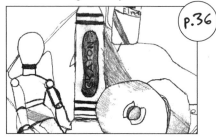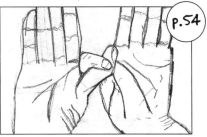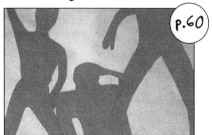

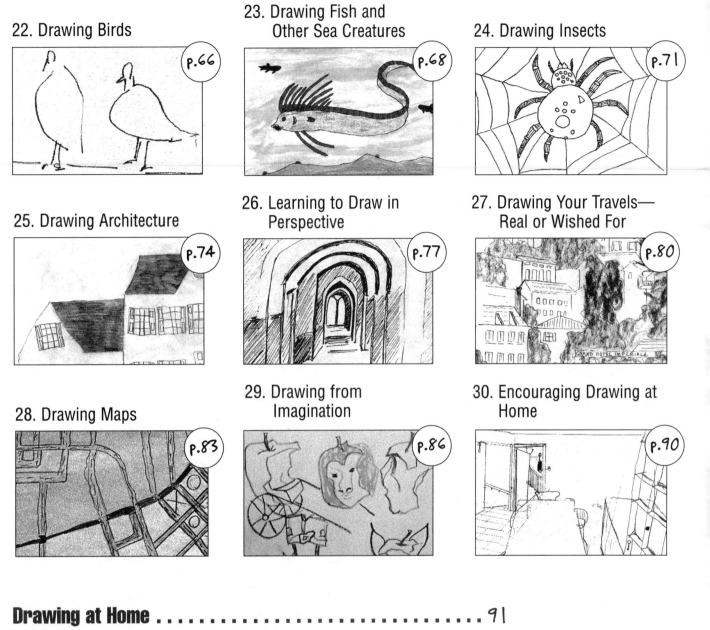

22. Drawing Birds p.66

23. Drawing Fish and Other Sea Creatures p.68

24. Drawing Insects p.71

25. Drawing Architecture p.74

26. Learning to Draw in Perspective p.77

27. Drawing Your Travels— Real or Wished For p.80

28. Drawing Maps p.83

29. Drawing from Imagination p.86

30. Encouraging Drawing at Home p.90

A Message to the Classroom Teacher

IT IS WITHIN THE POWERS OF EVERY PERSON TO DRAW.

Drawing is an essential means of expression, just as important as writing and oral expression in the daily work of learning. Drawing is a complementary mode of learning. It helps complete writing and verbal communication. Visual thinking is a dynamic element of learning. As a classroom teacher, you CAN teach visual thinking through drawing. It is important that you never draw for students but that you motivate them to look and to draw with their eyes. You can help them to see details and understand proportions, but the drawing is theirs.

Here are some important points to keep in mind about drawing.

❖ Drawing is as personal as handwriting. We all learn to shape cursive letters the same way. Yet, we each develop a unique style of handwriting that is our identification. Our drawing styles must be equally personal. Don't attempt to teach a student what something should look like; rather, teach how to look. All students will see uniquely, according to their levels of maturity and keenness of perception.

❖ When you teach perception, you are at the same time teaching reading. Reading begins with following a line of letters and looking carefully. Perceptual drawing helps develop that skill in a student.

❖ When children (or adults) draw by letting their eyes direct their hands, their concentration is beautiful. Try taking a drawing/writing break when your students are restless. It calms and centers them. Drawing is like meditation. Set the stage with quiet looking. When students start drawing "with their eyes," they will be very still and concentrated. They will go back to their other lessons relaxed and ready.

❖ Yes, there are artistically talented students, just as there are talented dancers, mathematicians, scientists, and so on. We would never accept the excuse, "I don't write beautifully, so I won't write." So, too, "I don't draw beautifully" is no excuse for not drawing. Third grade is a determining time for all natural-born artists who have drawn happily through their scribbling days—and this is just about every student. Too often children at this age begin to judge their drawing and decide that they "can't draw." Unfortunately, this fallacy continues throughout their lives. I have seen very bright students who will not draw. They have been so conditioned to getting the "right answer" that they find risking an "unsuccessful" drawing to be traumatic. Encouraging students to take risks is the most important lesson you can teach them. It will affect all of their learning.

❖ My experience with teachers as well as students has proven to me that linear thinking stifles individuals' drawing. Once empowered to risk "drawing with their eyes," in other words, really following edges with their eyes and letting the hand record them, everyone can draw. Try drawing your own shoe (see the directions on page 22) and trusting your eyes. More classroom teachers than I can count have done this exercise in my workshops and were so astounded at their drawings that they wanted to take them home and frame them. Often, these same teachers who believed they could not draw would have never initiated an art lesson in their classrooms.

❖ Drawing should be a means of expressing learning in every subject. The arts are unique in their potential to develop a healthy and productive attitude toward risk taking and learning from "failure"—the failure of creative ideas that stimulate new and better ideas.

❖ Howard Gardner's theory of multiple intelligences has extended our understanding of how we learn. Linguistic intelligence and logical-mathematical intelligence are only two facets of the mind through which we learn. Spatial intelligence, or the ability to perceive form and give visual shape to ideas, is of equal importance to many students. Some students respond much more readily to visual learning than to linear logic. The right-brain-dominant child will often resist a linear approach. Also, students whose family experiences have not encouraged reading and factual mastery will often be unprepared for the regimen of school but will draw happily and readily.

❖ Training students' eyes to really see is our first task as teachers. You, as a classroom teacher, should be a part of this visual learning. In an interdisciplinary learning climate, every subject should be approached both literally and expressively. A once-a-week art lesson by an art specialist cannot begin to reach these dimensions. Your help with developing students' basic drawing skills will enable the art specialist to move in leaps rather than slow steps.

Goals of Teaching Drawing

The real point about art education is that we must create whole human beings, people who are alive to their fingertips; people who are in a responsible attitude to sensation, to every organized form, to every meaning of the world about them. To open the closed eye is the first lesson of art in our time; the second is to open the inner eye, the eye of vision and dream.

—Lewis Mumford

❖ To develop in each student the skill and confidence to draw with his or her eyes so that he or she will be able to use drawing as a complementary and essential mode of learning in all subjects.

❖ To stimulate visual perception in every student.

❖ To teach students the language of art—how to look for lines, shapes, spaces, textures, and colors all around them.

❖ To make students aware of the principles of art—rhythm, balance, proportion—as they occur in movement and sound as well as in visual form.

❖ To nurture students' sensory perception through all their senses. Have them spend time touching, looking, listening, smelling, tasting, and then describing their perceptions.

❖ To spur the imaginations of your students, encouraging them to risk their ideas and create, invent, connect, experiment, and enjoy their own ideas.

❖ To allow yourself the joy of drawing, thus building your own confidence and your own vision.

Challenges You May Encounter

Most students at this age love to draw, and draw fearlessly, but you may encounter some of the following problems.

❖ **What about the student who will not draw certain kinds of images, such as figures?**
One girl I met said she did not draw figures; she drew trees. She would not even try to draw a figure. This is an example of the fear of risk taking that students who succeed in the "right answer" kind of testing often experience. By drawing trees, she could not meet her expectations for success. The most important lesson that such students need to learn is that taking risks and having failed attempts will enable them to discover new and better ways to succeed.

❖ **What about the student who draws fast and carelessly?**
Use the drawing/writing time to walk around and spot students who need guidance. Quiet concentration and observation need to be cultivated in today's fast-paced world and climate of passive entertainment. "Doing it yourself" needs nurturing in many students. Set the tone before giving the assignment. Prepare sketchbooks or other materials and tools. Model looking carefully at the object to be drawn. Encourage "crawling along every edge as if your eye is a bug."

❖ **What about the student who does not seem to see details?**
This may be a sign of a perceptual handicap such as dyslexia or some other related eye-hand dysfunction. Spend time with this student. Run your finger along the edge to be drawn. Then have the student do it. Much directed practice is needed. The better this student can discipline his or her eyes to follow an edge, the better he or she will read.

Drawing Is Basic

Drawing Is Basic is designed for daily fifteen-minute drawing and writing breaks carried out by the classroom teacher as a supplement to a full art curriculum. It is not an art curriculum. As a "drill" in perception, this program's goal is to make students comfortable with drawing objects and figures. Your students will be able to use this skill in all their subjects. The content of the drawing lessons provided here relates to all curriculum areas.

Set a time for drawing/writing. An effective plan is to set a time during your day when students typically need a break. Try to plan fifteen minutes each day. You will find that, when students draw, they become intensely quiet and involved. It frees them from the "response" mode and allows them to "express." Many times the drawing/writing break can be a part of a math, social studies, language arts, or science lesson.

With each drawing experience, a corresponding writing exercise is suggested. You may use other writing themes as well. Adapt and modify these drawing and writing ideas in whatever ways they fit your teaching and complement your curriculum.

Keep a journal. Encourage students to keep a notebook of their own in which they can write observations and ideas, and sketch small things that they observe each day. Occasionally take a few minutes to ask them to share an observation from their journals.

Plan. Work on one set of lessons for one to two weeks, depending on the number of lessons you choose to do. Some of the lessons will take longer than the fifteen-minute period. You might carry one through a week, working on it each day. During the first two weeks, you might concentrate on perceptual drawing lessons—drawing shoes, toys, and so on—and the sensory exercises. Continue these periodically throughout the school year.

Figure drawing will take many practice sessions. Have students do gesture drawings first, then contour drawings. Follow the sequence of lessons on drawing parts you can't see, drawing action, drawing groups, and so on. Do gesture-drawing exercises frequently. When students are secure in posing and drawing figures, they can use this skill to illustrate concepts in other subject matters.

Using the I Am an Artist Sketchbook

The student sketchbooks have a dual purpose.

1. The sketchbooks provide drawing paper for most of your lessons. However, you may want to have students draw on practice paper a few times before using the sketchbooks in some lessons. (For cutting lessons, you will want to provide other paper, such as construction paper.)

2. The sketchbooks also help you keep a record of students' development. Date pages as students complete them. Then periodically use the critiquing techniques beginning on page 18 to help students self-assess their work. Encourage students to keep sketchbooks through the years to see their growth.

Preparing Sketchbook Covers. The sketchbook covers are designed for students' self-portraits. Students can draw their self-portraits in the space provided on the cover, or use other creative ways to make this space their own.

Preparing for the Lessons

The greater the awareness of all the senses, the greater will be the opportunity for learning.

—Viktor Lowenfeld and Lambert W. Brittain

❖ Direct students to take their sketchbooks out, or distribute other paper. Select the drawing tool you want students to use, or allow them to choose their own.

❖ Introduce the lesson briefly. Then have students begin drawing. Observe students who are having trouble and help them to look carefully at their subjects. Do not draw for them.

❖ Direct students to let their eyes crawl like a bug along each edge, moving from one edge to another as they touch. Direct them to let their hands just follow the path of their eyes, noting every line and detail.

❖ Tell students that they may look at their papers whenever they need to but that they should not draw again until their eyes are on the objects. They may extend lines to close shapes in their drawings, but they should look back at their subjects before continuing to draw.

❖ Encourage drawing a flowing line rather than several sketchy lines. The eye and hand will not work together if one is moving along and the other is not.

❖ Don't be satisfied with tiny little drawings or drawings done without looking. A quick circle for an apple is not a perceptual drawing. Take time to hold an apple up and ask for descriptions of its shape.

❖ At the end of each lesson, allow four or five minutes for students to write a sentence or two about their drawing experiences or about the subjects of their drawings. Share these writings periodically by having students read them aloud.

Stretch your imagination to its limits and it will dance.

Tools and Materials

Drawing Tools

Each drawing tool has its own potential and characteristics. This drawing program focuses on the basic tools, but even these offer a wide range of possibilities of line quality and texture. Vary the tools your students use in the daily exercises. Encourage them to experiment with each tool.

Drawing with pencil. For best results, use an ebony pencil for drawing. It has dark, soft lead and can make a whole range of tones from black to gray. Experiment with it by pressing heavily or lightly. Show students how to hold the pencil on its side to make thick and thin lines. Here is a gray scale done with an ebony pencil. Have your students measure a 1" × 8" rectangle and try their own gray scales.

Drawing with crayon.
Encourage students to try pressing heavily or lightly as they draw with crayons. You might have them create watercolor resist over hard waxy lines and shapes.

Drawing with charcoal.
Charcoal pencils or sticks of charcoal offer a different medium, one that can be blended and smudged for interesting effects. Offer charcoal as an alternative drawing tool.

Here are four drawings done with pencil, marker, crayon, and charcoal. Compare the qualities of each of these media.

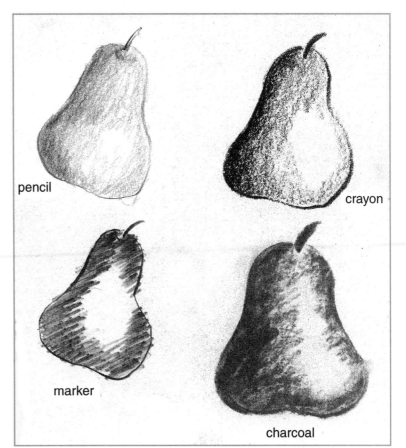

pencil

crayon

marker

charcoal

Experimenting with tools. Use a drawing break to experiment with each tool. Ask students to draw lines that are

ANGULAR THIN *flowing* *scribbly* BOLD *Graceful* **THICK**

Ask students to think of more adjectives and draw to illustrate what the words sound like or mean to them.

Drawing Materials

Materials for drawing include paper of different sizes and weights. The student sketchbooks will provide drawing paper for most lessons; however, provide students with other paper for practice. Some lessons call for larger sheets of paper, 12" × 18" or 18" × 24." Kraft/mural paper is a good, economical choice. Use mural paper and overhead projectors to enlarge shapes and figures for murals.

For cutting activities, construction paper, scissors, and glue will be needed. For crayon resist, paintbrushes, watercolors, and plastic cups of water will be needed.

Classroom Resources

A classroom that is visually exciting is a stimulus to looking, learning, and expressing. There are numerous resources, both for purchase and free, that can add visual energy to your classroom. Display various objects in your classroom and encourage students to pick them up, examine them, and feel them. Here are some ideas for creating a climate that stimulates visual learning in your classroom.

❖ Have a place for found objects—stones, small branches, a wheel from a broken toy, and the many things that children like to collect. This will be a source of ideas for drawing. Place these objects in a box or on a small table.

❖ Make nature photographs, videos, and math manipulatives available. Tapes of educational television programs can provide rich resources. Pause videos to allow students to look carefully at birds, animals, flowers, and so on. Study shapes and colors of fish, zebras, and other forms, as well as patterns on them.

❖ Create a texture board or box. Encourage students to bring in pieces of cloth, paper, or other things with textured surfaces. Develop vocabulary by describing the textures.

❖ Borrow birds, boxes of butterflies, and other natural objects from your local nature museum.

❖ Visit zoos, museums, and other exhibits with students to stimulate their interest in recording what they see. Encourage students to use their sketchbooks on these visits.

❖ Encourage students to take their sketchbooks and journals on family trips and to draw what they see.

❖ Invite students to bring family ethnic costumes or memorabilia to class. Have students pose with their costumes or objects while other students draw them.

Critiquing Techniques

Do each of the exercises several times with students. Each experience of looking intently at objects to be drawn will sharpen students' perception and improve their drawing. Periodically, allow time for your students to review their drawings and critique their own progress. Encourage honest criticism, both positive and negative.

It is important to establish a climate for positive criticism in your classroom. Here are some ideas to accomplish this. You might say,

❖ This drawing exercise is "eye training," not just sketching. We are training our eyes to look more carefully and our hands to work with our eyes.

❖ If you risk not getting it "right," your drawing skills will get better and better. If you don't try, your skills won't improve.

❖ Critiquing our work means looking at it to see if it could be better. It is the best way to improve our skills.

❖ We are helping each other when we offer constructive criticism. We are helping ourselves when we decide what could be better in our drawings.

❖ Remember, your drawing is just as much your own as your handwriting. Don't try to copy someone else's drawing. Be confident of your own talents and abilities.

❖ As your sketchbook fills up, go back and compare your early drawings with your new ones to see the improvement.

The Elements of Art

The elements of art—line, shape, texture, color, and space—are like parts of speech in language. They are what you use as you draw, and each element has expressive power. Ask students to look for the following elements of art in their drawings.

Line. Have students talk about lines in their drawings. Ask if their lines are thick, thin, flowing, or angular. Talk about how drawing tools affect lines.

Shape. Direct students to look at the shapes of the objects they drew. Do their drawings look like the objects? Ask them to explain how they drew the shapes of the objects. Did they change the shapes to show something unique about how they saw the objects?

Texture. Did students find a way to show how the objects they drew feel? Describe textures, such as soft, hard, fuzzy, or hairy. How did students show the textures of the objects?

Color. If students used color in their drawings, ask how it added to their drawings. Suggest that if they draw a red apple, they use a red crayon to draw its shape as well as its color.

Space. If students' drawings show space in a room or a landscape, ask how they showed it. Did they draw things smaller in the distance? Did they draw objects behind other objects by showing only the parts they could see? Teach foreground, middle ground, and background.

The Principles of Art

The principles of art are the "rules" for organizing elements in artworks. Present the following principles of art to students.

Rhythm. Ask your students to tap out rhythms on their desks, such as A, BB, A, BB. Rhythm is a pattern that comes from repetition. Point out repeat rows of design, repeat colors, and so on, to students. Help them recognize other examples of visual rhythm.

Balance and Proportion. These principles of art create a pleasing order of size and arrangement of forms in a composition. Teach symmetry, bilateral and radial.

Variety. Teach students to recognize and appreciate the differences, or variety, in shapes, colors, textures, lines, and so on.

Unity. Help students understand the concept of a harmonious composition in which all the principles of art are working together.

Assessment

This program is designed as a drill in perception, not as a subject to be graded. Make assessment a positive experience. Encourage students to assess their own progress by asking them to compare recent drawings with those completed earlier, and to find ways in which they are improving. Keep and date drawings, especially those in the student sketchbooks, as a means of both teacher and individual assessment. To keep track of students' monthly progress during the school year, duplicate the chart on page 96 for each student. A sample is shown below.

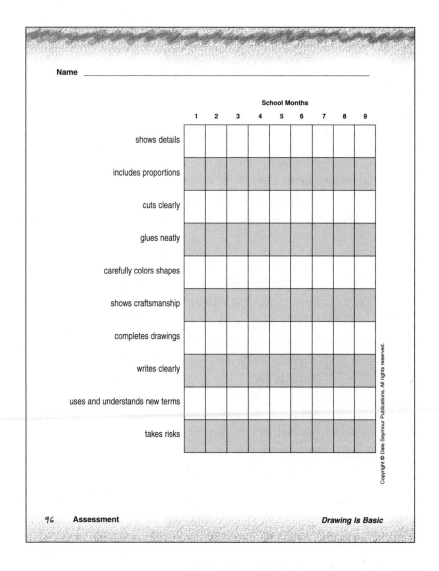

Name _____

School Months

	1	2	3	4	5	6	7	8	9
shows details									
includes proportions									
cuts clearly									
glues neatly									
carefully colors shapes									
shows craftsmanship									
completes drawings									
writes clearly									
uses and understands new terms									
takes risks									

96   Assessment   *Drawing Is Basic*

21

Drawing Exercises

All of the following drawing exercises are written as you would present them to your students. Directions and suggestions for you, the teacher, are in italic type. The ✏ icon indicates teacher dialogue.

I. Daily Exercises in Perception

Create a climate of looking thoughtfully before students begin drawing.

✏ Train your eyes to follow every edge of whatever you are drawing. Your eyes will direct your hand. *(Distribute a kernel of popped corn to each student.)* Look carefully at the kernel. Follow an edge until it disappears. Then pick up another edge. Continue drawing until you have drawn every edge you see. This is called **contour** drawing. Write a description of the shape you have drawn.

You might want to have students draw shoes on practice paper a few times before they draw in their sketchbooks. Encourage students to save their drawings so that they can compare and critique their own work. Tools: pencils (no eraser), crayons, or markers. Draw shoes many times, looking for top, side, back, and bottom views.

✏ Take off one shoe. Before drawing, turn your shoe around to see how different it looks from each angle. Run your finger along the lines and decorative details of the shoe. Place the shoe at the top of your desk, and your paper flat on your desk in front of it. Start drawing at the top back of the shoe, letting your eyes move along the edge toward the front. Draw as large as you can. As your eyes move along, let your hand and tool follow the movement. Draw a flowing line.

Look back at your drawing when you need to, but stop drawing when you do. You may want to extend a line to meet and close a shape, but do not start drawing again until your eyes are where you left off on your shoe. Draw every detail you see on your shoe—lines for the sole, laces, and so on.

When you have finished, turn the shoe in a different position and draw another view of it. Draw several different views of many different kinds of shoes. Choose a drawing tool that will work well for each type of shoe. Write a sales pitch to sell your shoes.

Compare these student drawings of shoes. Each drawing is individual. Each student sees and records details differently. Look for that uniqueness and applaud it in each student's work.

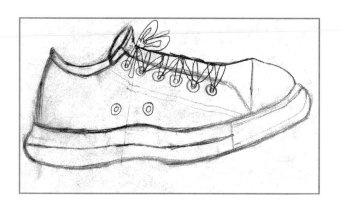

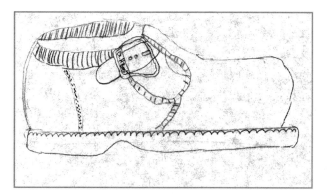

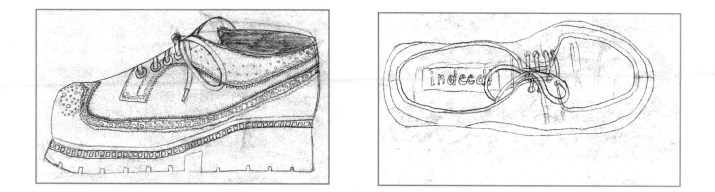

✏ Design a pair of shoes you would like to wear. Draw a side view and a front view. Describe the material, the color, and the design of your shoes.

✏ Smash an aluminum soda can and draw it just as it looks. Follow every edge with your eye. Draw the distorted lettering on the can. Write about recycling.

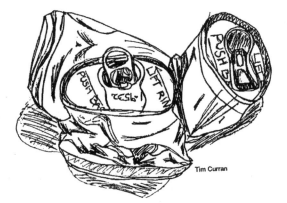
Tim Curran

✏ Draw a pair of gloves. Toss them on the desk in a rumpled shape and draw every line. Write about the kinds of materials that gloves are made of and which materials work best in different climates.

✏ Draw your pencil box and its contents. How would you make a pencil? How does the lead get inside the wood? Write about it.

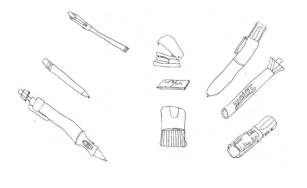

✏ Draw a stack of your schoolbooks. Start at the bottom and draw each one as you see it. Try turning some of them at an angle.

✏ Collect miniature cars and other small toys. Choose one toy and draw it in detail. Write sentences describing your toy.

Tim Curran

✏ Draw your legs and feet on a skateboard. Write about how it feels to fly along on one.

✏ Bring a musical instrument to class and draw all of its parts. Write about music you like.

2. Drawing in 3-D

Prepare for the 3-D approach to drawing by having students handle objects, turn them around, and notice their roundness and other variations of shape on all sides.

✏ Draw a glass or other cylindrical container. Look carefully at the shape of the base and the top. See and draw the curve that shows its volume. Study this student's drawing of a wine goblet. Notice the shadow tones the student drew. This is called *chiaroscuro*. Look up the definition of chiaroscuro and write about how it is used. Find drawings by Rembrandt to see his masterful use of chiaroscuro.

✏ Draw a pinecone. Study the way its parts spread out and overlap. Start at one end and just keep your eye on each part as you draw. Draw slowly and thoughtfully. Research and write about how the seeds in a pinecone are spread to start new trees.

✏ Draw a bottle. Look at the shape of the base of the bottle and the neck. Show the roundness in your lines. Find and draw the shadows. Write about how glass is blown into bottle shapes.

✏ This drawing of a carved wood tripod is by a sixth-grade student. Notice how carefully its three parts are interlocked. Find a three-dimensional object and draw it so that you show its depth. Then write a description of the object you drew.

3. Connecting to All of Your Senses

✏ Make a list of adjectives. Draw a page of lines that look like each adjective. *(Suggest that students place all three drawing tools on the desk and then, for each adjective, choose one that will work best.)*

Prepare the following lesson by putting small objects, such as empty toothpaste tubes, shells, golf balls, kernels of popcorn, and bottle caps in brown paper lunch bags. Distribute one bag to each student.

✏ Do not look in the bag. Use your senses. Feel an object in the bag with one hand as you draw it with the other. Feel all of the edges and draw what they feel like. Don't just identify your object. Write about it when you have finished drawing it.

✏ *(Distribute a small rock to each student.)* Use your memory. Look carefully at your rock for a full minute. Now put it away and draw all the details you remember. When you have finished, compare your drawing with the rock and write about all that you have learned.

✏ Use all of your senses. Think about a hot dog just the way you like to eat it. Write ten adjectives that describe it. Now draw it large in your sketchbook, including all the "trimmings."

This is a student's drawing of a hot dog.

4. Drawing Flowers

Distribute one real or artificial flower to each student. Teach the parts of a flower, so students will find and draw the pistil, stamen, petal, sepal, stem, and leaves.

✐ Draw a **radially symmetrical** flower, such as a daisy. Try to draw the petals so they look like they are soft. Draw a second row of petals behind the first row. Think about the shape of the leaves and the bend of the stem. Describe the flower.

✐ Design a flower arrangement with just five flowers and a few carefully placed leaves and branches. Write about why you selected the flower shapes in your arrangement.

✐ Plant a carrot in a glass of water and watch the roots develop. Draw a sequence of growth sketches. Keep a diary of the progress of roots, stem, and leaves. *(You might ask students to do this at home over a period of a few weeks and draw many stages of the growth.)*

Place a plant in the center of the room so desks can be turned toward it. Each student will have a different view. Compare views when finished.

✐ Draw a potted plant. Let your eyes wander along every vein and line of every leaf and stem. Follow each leaf right to its tip. Notice leaves that are behind other leaves. Draw just what you can see. Draw the plant's container, too. If you drew a plant in fifth grade, compare the drawings to see how much you have improved. Write about how you see the plant parts. This is one student's drawing.

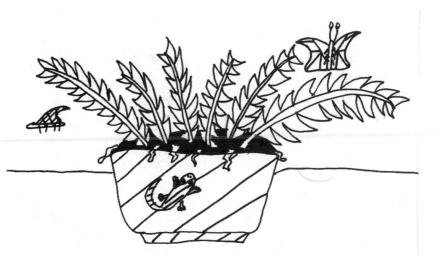

- Celebrate the tiny things in nature. Find a very small flower, shell, or insect. Draw it on a large sheet of paper, making it as large as you can.

- Find photographs of tropical flowers and draw them. Use colored markers to capture their vibrant colors.

- Do a contour-line drawing of a flower. This one is a tiger lily. It was drawn with a soft ebony pencil, using the point to draw the fine outlines of the petals and the side to get shadow tones. Notice how the leaves curl and twist. Find a real or artificial flower and draw it. Write a haiku about a flower. Haiku is a Japanese form of poetry that has seventeen syllables—five in the first line, seven in the second line, and five in the last line. *(Read aloud the following haiku written by a student.)*

Spreading its petals
Reaching for the sun's warm rays
Elegant lily

5. Drawing Trees

The growth pattern called organic branching is found in so many forms in nature. Start with a bulletin board of branching forms. Ask your students to bring in pictures or diagrams of everything from a small twig to the pattern of blood vessels in the body. Lightning branches. Cracks in the sidewalk branch. Rivers branch. Connect this to geography. Each species of tree has a unique branching pattern. Send students to the library, the Internet, books, and magazines to find and gather pictures of many species of trees.

✏ *(Take students outside on a nice day with pencils and sketchbooks. Find a tree and tell students to start at the base and "climb up the trunk with their eyes.")* Pretend your eye is a bug crawling up the tree. Follow the line out to a branch. See it connect to a smaller branch. Bring the line back, and give the branch thickness. Keep your eyes on the tree. Note the lines of branches going behind other branches. Practice different ways of drawing foliage. You might draw each leaf, scribble clusters of leaves, or build up many tiny lines to make a large mass. Foliage can be drawn in many ways. Note these students' drawings and the different solutions they used to draw foliage. This is a sure sign that the students were really looking.

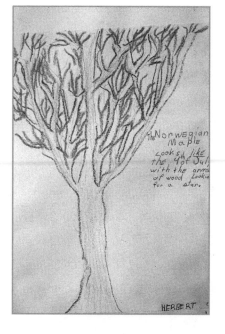

✏ Study trees on your way home from school. Look for many different branching patterns. Some trees branch upward while others bend down. Pine trees branch out horizontally. Notice the main branches and then the smaller branches on each of the larger branches. No two trees are alike. Find patterns you like and draw them.

✏ Draw a row of trees starting at the bottom of your paper. Now start about 2 inches up and draw trees behind the trees you drew, but for this second row draw only what will be seen of them. Think of ten words to describe a dense wooded area.

✏ Read Robert Frost's poem "The Road Not Taken." It describes a forest and a road that divides into two paths. Find words describing the woods and the paths. Draw your image of it. Note the descriptions of the undergrowth on one path and of the other, grassy path. Then talk about what Frost meant by this poem.

✏ Write a diamante poem about your tree. This is a poem having seven lines and forming a diamond shape.

Show the format of a diamante poem, like this:

One noun
Two adjectives
Three participles
Four nouns related to the first
Three participles (showing change)
Two adjectives
One noun (opposite of the first)

This is an example of a diamante poem.

Winter

bitter, gray

freezing, slipping, sliding

snow, slush, rain, sunshine

melting, warming, blooming

happy, sunny

summer

✐ Bring a beautiful leaf to class. First do a rubbing with the veined side under your paper. Now use the branching pattern of the leaf to draw a large plant. Add leaves and flowers to the branches.

✐ Here is a pencil drawing of a tree in Yellowstone National Park. It is growing on the side of a steep cliff, and its roots are clinging to the cliff. Imagine your own tree with roots forming a secure base. Draw the tree and its roots. Write about people's roots.

6. Drawing Textures

There are two kinds of textures in art—actual and simulated. Actual is texture you can feel—like that of a drawing made from yarn glued to paper. Simulated texture is drawn to look like a texture, such as fuzzy, smooth, rough, and so on.

✏ Use a glue dispenser to "draw" lines on your paper in the shape of a tree. Lay yarn or string on your glue lines and make a tree that you can "see" with your fingers. Close your eyes and feel it. Then write about how much your fingers told you when your eyes couldn't see.

✏ Now do a drawing of a simulated texture. This drawing by a sixth grader shows the fuzzy quality of a teddy bear. Notice how she used many short lines to show the furriness and a smooth gray for the nose. Describe the look and feel of the object you draw.

✏ Draw a robot figure and fill in all the parts with a texture by rubbing with crayon over grids and other rough surfaces. Write an ad to sell your robot as a household helper.

✏ Collect shells, seeds from maple trees, acorns, and other small objects. Draw each one, trying to show the texture. Think of many adjectives to describe texture. *(This is a drawing of a shell by a sixth-grade student.)*

32

✐ This drawing of tree-covered hills is by a sixth-grade student. Study the many tiny lines that represent trees, a rocky road, and the flow of water. Create your own landscape drawing with many textures. Write a diamante poem about it. *(See page 30.)*

7. Drawing Food

Bring fresh vegetables and fruits to class. Bunches of carrots, endive or leaf lettuce, bunches of radishes or individual radishes with their leaves, pears, apples, bananas, and bunches of grapes all have interesting shapes. Take time to talk about them and look carefully at their shapes, colors, and textures.

☞ *(Display celery stalks.)* Draw a stalk of celery. Look for overlapping pieces and for the string like lines on each piece. Draw the leaves and show them overlapping. Make up a recipe for cooking celery. It could be a soup.

☞ *(Provide a chart or a food pyramid of the four basic food groups.)* Draw four compositions made up of foods from each of the basic food groups— fruits and vegetables, dairy products, meats and fish, and grains. Choose your favorite foods for each composition. Write about planning a balanced meal. *(Connect this with a science lesson on nutrition. Ask students to list many examples of each food group.)*

☞ *(Display a head of curly lettuce.)* Draw lettuce leaves. Pretend they are dancing figures. Try to catch the rhythm of the movement. Describe the dance.

✏ *(Display some apples.)* Study the shape of an apple. It has a very graceful curve. Look at the stem and the bottom. Turn the apple and look at it from different views. Look for lights and shadows on the apple's shape. Draw a group of three apples. Write a description of the apples. Use adjectives to describe their color, shape, smell, and taste. This is a student's drawing of three apples. Note the shadows.

✏ Bring fruits to school to represent each color of the color wheel. For example, red apples, yellow pears, green limes, and purple grapes. Draw them in a color wheel formation.

✏ *(Display a head of red cabbage. Cut into it.)* Draw the many lines you see. This drawing was created by a student. Write about what the lines of the cabbage could look like—water rushing in a stream?

Eat $mart . . .

Have a Cabbage

8. Learning Composition

Composition *is the arrangement of forms. A good composition should include the*
following principles of art.

Balance.
Balance can be symmetrical or asymmetrical. Bilaterally
symmetrical means the composition has equally sized shapes on each side of
its center.

Proportion and Variety.
The relation of shapes and colors to each
other in a composition can be realistically proportional or exaggerated. A
variety of lines, shapes, and colors adds interest to a composition.

Rhythm.
In art, rhythm is an ordered movement created by repetition of
color, shape, line, and other elements of art. Objects in a composition can be
drawn ***overlapping*** *with one behind another to create repetition and rhythm.*

Unity.
When all the principles of art work together, they create unity, or a
pleasing composition.

Foreground/Middle Ground/Background.
Foreground
means the objects or shapes drawn; middle ground is the objects behind the
foreground shapes; background is the space all around these objects. Think of
background as shape also. In a landscape, the ***horizon line*** *marks the*
background. Drawing a room, you will find the floor line.

✎ This is an asymmetrical
landscape drawn by a
sixth-grade student.
Notice how the tree on
the left balances the
road leading off the
right side. Draw your
own asymmetrical
landscape. Include
trees, a fence, hills,
perhaps a lake.

✏ Draw a bilaterally symmetrical composition of bottles. Start in the center with a tall form. Then add the same forms to each side to get a pleasing arrangement. Add texture by doing rubbings on the bottle forms or on the background with a crayon over a textured surface. Write an evaluation of your composition.

Set up a still-life arrangement—a group of objects placed together. Set it in the center of the room so that everyone sees it from a different view.

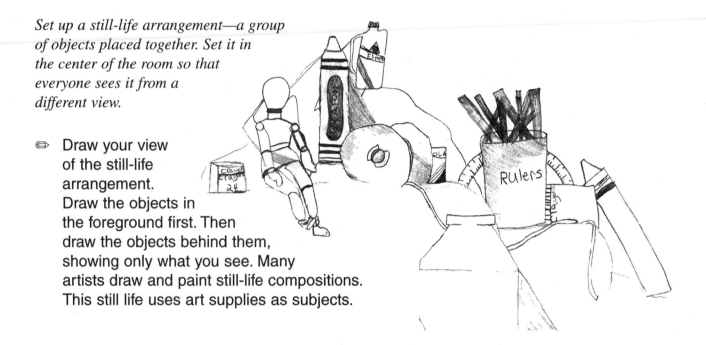

✏ Draw your view of the still-life arrangement. Draw the objects in the foreground first. Then draw the objects behind them, showing only what you see. Many artists draw and paint still-life compositions. This still life uses art supplies as subjects.

✏ Use a marker to divide your page into sections. Then pattern each section to make a pleasing and balanced composition. Here are two students' examples.

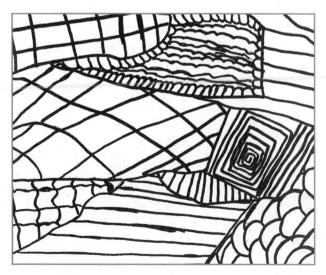

9. Composing with Imaginary Lines

*Teach **topography**—the study of the relief features of a surface, such as mountains, roads, and rivers on the earth.*

✏ Space drawings of five small stone shapes on your paper. Then start on the left side of your paper and draw many lines like flowing water across your paper, letting your lines "flow" around the stones. Write a poem about your drawing.

✏ *(Arrange a coat or a small blanket in a heap on a table.)* Look at the lines of folds. Holding your paper horizontally, draw the lines you see starting from the left edge. Use crayons in earth colors. If a line disappears, draw the line that overlaps it. When you have five or six lines drawn, look at your drawing and visualize a landscape. Add trees, roads, and more color to complete the view. Write about where your landscape is located—perhaps the desert, or a mountain range. Study this drawing of folds. Can you see a landscape drawing that could be made from it?

10. Composing with Math Tools

The ruler, compass, and protractor are good tools for drawing. Students can develop their skills in measuring and manipulation of the tools when using them to draw.

✏ Use a ruler to draw ten diagonal lines on the sketchbook page. Then draw lines to connect parts and divide the design into sections. Complete sections with more straight lines, using markers in many different colors. Write your own version of the directions for another exercise like this one.

✏ Use the compass to draw a 6-inch circle. Using the radius set on your compass, mark the circumference into six sections. Draw lines to make a hexagon. Add other circles or lines to complete your design.

✏ Draw a large circle. From the same center point, draw smaller, **concentric circles**. Draw repeated patterns in each section. Use markers to give your design strength. Write about three circular objects that you use at school or at home.

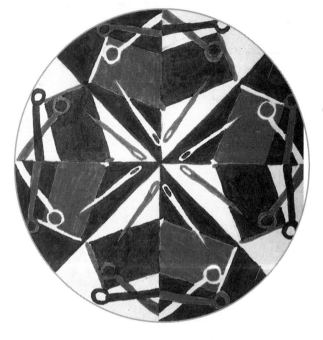

✏ Divide a 7-inch diameter circle into halves, quarters, and eighths. Make a design in each section. Here is a student's design using scissors and needles. Write about your design ideas.

✏ Shapes can be organic—shapes and forms from nature, or geometric—having angles and sharp edges. Create two designs; one with all organic shapes and another with all geometric shapes. Compare them.

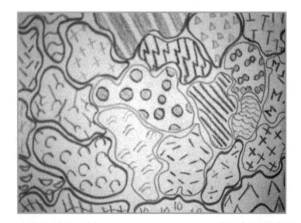

✏ On the flap of a business envelope, design the letters of your name into a geometric pattern. Use crayon or marker colors to make your design interesting. Be sure the letters are clear and legible. Arrange the envelopes on a bulletin board titled "Our Post Office" and encourage students to write letters to each other.

✏ A **tessellation** is a design made of repeated shapes with no space between them. Tile floors, for example, can be tessellations of squares, rectangles, and hexagons. Design a tessellation. Start with a 2" square. *(Display the diagram below, demonstrating each step.)* (1) Cut a small shape from one side. (2) Slide this shape to the opposite side and tape the uncut edges together. (3) Cut another shape from a third side. (4) Slide this shape to the opposite side and tape the uncut edges together. On a 12" × 18" sheet of paper, begin tracing your shape carefully. After the first tracing, use the existing line to continue. Fill the paper with these shapes. Then, using a marker, outline the shapes and add details to make them into something else. Use several colors to make your tessellation interesting. Write about this process of imagining.

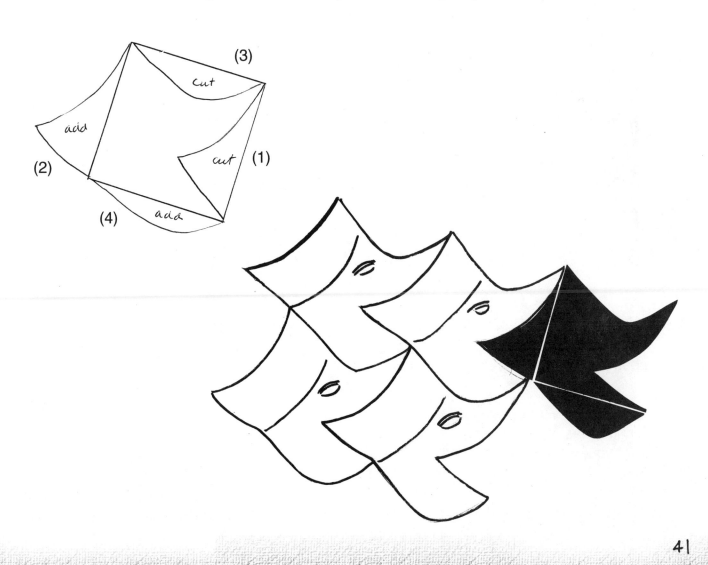

11. Composing on a Computer

Computer drawing programs are very useful for developing awareness of line quality, direction, and tone. Using different software programs, students can experiment with thick and thin lines, line directions, repetition of lines and shapes, composition, and tonality. Here are three beginning exercises.

✏ Use many different kinds of lines to make a pleasing composition in a computer drawing program. Repeat lines and shapes to create rhythm. Try to achieve balance—either symmetrical or asymmetrical—in your composition. Look at the proportions of large and small forms. Describe the effect.

✏ Experiment with wash tones using a computer drawing program to learn about shadow effects. Combine lines and washes in a composition about the weather. Write a haiku about rain or fog.

✏ Scan one of your drawings and then experiment with tone and texture within areas of the drawing. Try many ways until you are satisfied. Then print your work. Write about the experience of taking risks with your ideas.

12. Drawing the Human Figure

This skill is essential. Do not accept stick figures. Once your students feel confident posing for each other and drawing gestures, you can apply this skill for further expression in any and all of their studies. Here are some things to look for when you critique students' figure drawings.

Proportion/Size and Relation of Parts. *Is the head too large for the body? Are the arms long enough? Do the elbows come to the waist? How far down do the hands reach? The better students understand the way the body works, the better they will be able to draw it.*

Measurements. *Most adult bodies are about seven heads high. Children's bodies are much less than that. Measure your model's head and then see how many heads tall he or she is.*

Details. *Did students draw hands and feet? In a full contour drawing, did they draw features in the face or details of clothing?*

Movement. *Do students' figures look as if they could move an arm or a leg? Are they too stiff?*

Line. *Do students hatch their lines instead of letting them flow? Remind them to let their lines follow the paths of their eyes.*

Use a cardboard Halloween skeleton or a small plastic model to study the structure of the human body. Show students the head and how the neck continues into the backbone as well as the shoulder bones and the two straight arm bones with ball joints at the shoulders. You might compare the way this joint moves to the way a joystick moves. Have students demonstrate that their elbows come to their waists and their hands to their midthighs. Point out the skeleton's hipbones and the two straight leg bones connected to the hip with ball joints. Have students feel these bones in their own bodies.

✏ Do a gesture drawing from a posed model and fill in the bones. Think about the skull, backbone, ribs, shoulder bones, hipbones, joints, hands, and feet. Describe how the body moves—the marvelous way our bones and muscles allow us to do so many things.

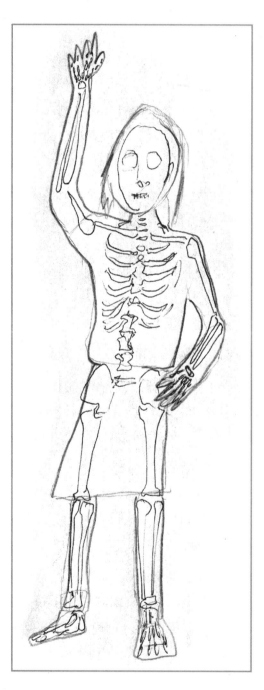

Gesture Drawing

To teach gesture drawing, tell students to look only at the outline of the body—not the details. Start with a student model in front of the room in a simple pose with both arms akimbo (hands on hips and elbows bent outward) or one akimbo and one upraised. Direct students to start with the oval of the head. Use practice paper for students' first gesture drawings.

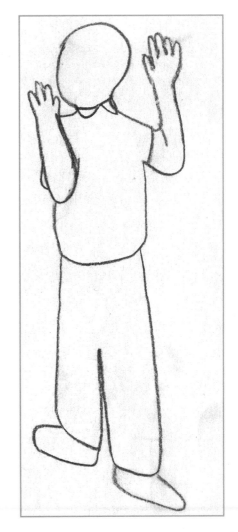

✏ Keeping your eyes on the model, follow the line from the head to one side of the neck, to the shoulder, to the arm—both straight sections—around the hand, up the inside of the arm to the body, down to the waist, to the hip, to the knee, to the foot, and up the inside of the leg. Continue around the body until your line reaches the other side of the neck.

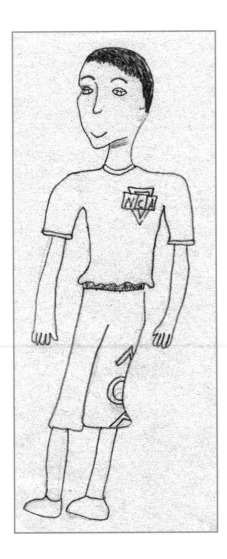

Have students do many gesture sketches, taking time to look at the results for proportions and body parts. Keep to frontal poses while students are getting comfortable with the figure. Point out that students on opposite sides of the room will see the model differently. Change models for each pose.

- Suggest poses for your model—reaching, bending, stretching, climbing, and so on. Do several quick gesture drawings to get a good feeling for the proportions of the body. Write a brief story about one of your drawings.

Have a model sit on a chair, stand at a chair with one foot on the seat, or sit on the floor. Ask students to think of a pose that hides some parts of the model from view.

- How do you draw a head or a body that is bent down or turned around? Or an arm that is behind the body or bent away from your view? Trust your eyes. Draw only what you see. Do many poses like this. Write about what you learn.

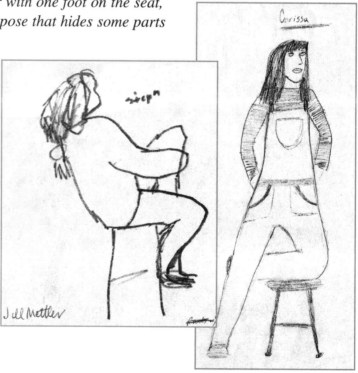

- Draw a figure from a posed model with the arms slightly away from the body. Cut out your drawing and use it as a paper doll. Design clothes for it. Write commercials to sell your clothing designs.

✏ Try drawing a back view. Pose your model sitting on a chair with his or her back to the class. Draw as much of the arms and legs and face as you can see from your view.

✏ Have your model pose in an open doorway, reaching out to touch the sides of the door frame. Start your drawing at the door frame and draw only the negative spaces around the model. This is a student example.

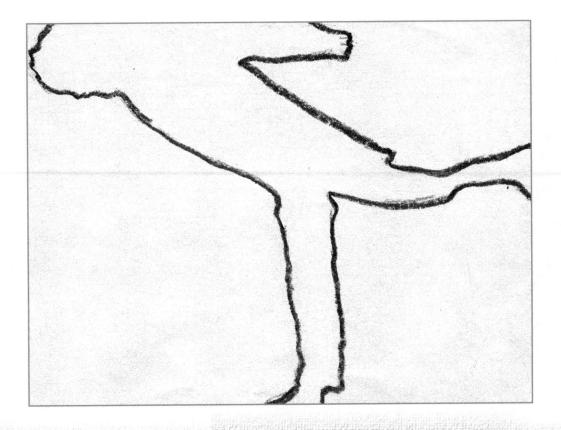

13. It Looks Different from Every Angle

✏ *(Position the model in the center of the room so students can see the pose from all different angles.)* Draw the model. Compare views when you have finished. Write about how you saw the model. These student drawings show four views of the same model.

Ashley McKay

Elizabeth Moeykens

moeykens

This drawing of many views and actions was done by a student after having attended a performance by the London Symphony Orchestra. Study the drawing for figure action and for composition. Try to draw several views in one composition. Write about the kind of music you enjoy.

Stonke Anthony Ferris

14. Capturing Action

✏ Your models won't always be sitting or standing still for you. Let's look at models who are moving. How can your lines capture that movement? Draw your models in actions, like dancing. Try to show the movement with your lines and shapes. Here is an exciting student drawing of action. Describe the action of your model.

✏ Have a model pose in four stages of a movement. Draw all four poses in sequence to show the action. Write about what you learned from doing this.

✏ *(Have models pose using gestures suggesting emotions—excitement, fear, or even anger.)* Write about what the person in your drawing might be thinking.

15. Drawing Faces

Teach the proportions of the face. Begin by drawing an oval on the board. Then measure the oval from top to bottom and draw a line across the midpoint. Help students discover that the eyes are in the middle of the skull and that the ears are level with the eyes. Have students come up and draw eyes, eyebrows, ears, a nose, a mouth, and the hairline. Then measure a young child's face and point out that the proportions are different—the eyes are much lower and the forehead is larger.

✏ Face a partner and draw a front view of his or her face.

1. Start with the oval of the head. Look at the chin line. Is it pointed, round, or square?

2. Measure from the top of the head to the chin and lightly mark the halfway point. Draw the eyes here. Look at the eyelids and eyelashes. Look closely at the iris of each eye. The eyelid will cover about a third of it unless the person is staring wide-eyed. Draw the pupils of the eyes.

3. Draw the eyebrows. Feel on your own face how they lead to the nose. The nose will come about halfway down the lower half of the face. Draw the nostrils and the end of the nose.

4. Draw the mouth.

5. Draw the ears. They are even with the eyes.

6. Draw the hairline and the shape of the hair.

7. Finally, draw the neck and shoulders.

✏ Draw many faces, looking each time at details and proportions. Describe your model's features.

✏ Draw a self-portrait. Look in a mirror and find the shape of your face, the lines of your eyebrows, your hairline and the style of your hair, and so on. Create a verbal self-portrait by describing yourself in words.

✏ Draw a profile of your partner. Let your eyes direct your hand. Look closely at the shape of the forehead, the angle of the nose, and the shape of the lips and chin. Do this many times until you are drawing profiles with ease.

By Natalie Callaghan

Avery

✏ Study this charcoal self-portrait by the German artist Kathe Kollwitz.
   She used the side of the charcoal to blend tones and shadows.

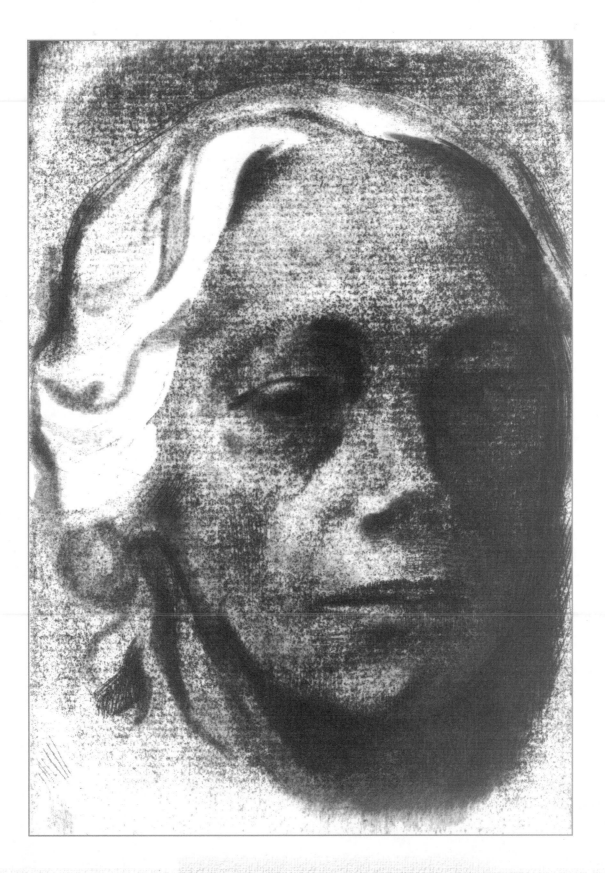

16. Drawing Details of the Body

✏ Draw your hand from two views. Put your thumb and index finger together for one view. Write about all the things that pressing these two fingers together allows you to do. This student drew thumbs intertwined.

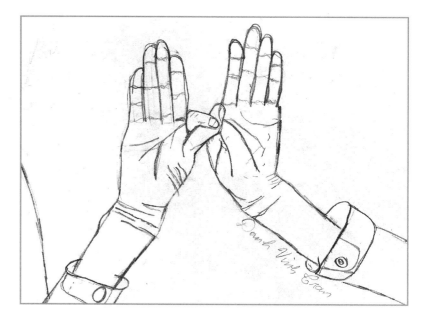

✏ Look down at your leg and foot. This artist drew his leg and bare foot. Draw yours, but with your shoe and sock. Write about how your shoe feels to the touch.

✏ Look carefully at the ear of the student next to you. Draw the ear with every detail. Let your eyes follow each line and curve. Write about your favorite sounds.

✏ Pair off and draw your partner's hairline. Follow every line you see—curly, straight, wavy, or whatever hairline you see. Draw the side, front, and back views.

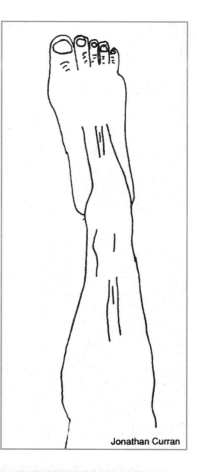

Jonathan Curran

17. Contour Drawing

Discuss with students the importance of trusting their own vision and not trying to draw like someone else. Remind them to just keep trying to see better and to draw what they see. Then discuss the confidence that each student should have in his or her own work.

✏ Now that you have drawn the gestures of the body and the way its parts move together, you are ready to see the figure as artists see it—finding all the edges as they move across the body and the way they disappear when other edges cross over them. You are ready to do contour drawing of figures.

(You might ask students to write the following in their journals for reference.)
Contour drawing is a very sensitive search for all the lines you can see. Let your eyes follow the line of the collar, the folds and creases of the clothing, and the lines of the face and hair. Do contour drawing more slowly than gesture drawing. Enjoy all the lines and the way they disappear as another fold overlaps. Think of contour drawing as walking across a landscape with hills and valleys. Your eyes find "paths," and your pen records them.

✏ Take some time to "draw with your finger." Look at the model and, with one eye closed, trace with your finger the edges you see. Follow the line of a collar around the neck and to the front. Find the lines of folds, pleats, and decorations on your model's clothes. Then draw as your eyes "feel" each line. Write about the path your eyes took. This is a student's example of contour drawing.

A student drew this portrait of her teacher in pencil. Draw a full-length portrait of your teacher or a friend. Write a note to him or her to accompany the portrait.

18. Finding Subjects in Your Studies

✐ Study the ancient Egyptian style of drawing figures. The ancient Egyptians drew the broadest view of each part of the body—the profile of the head, the front view of the eyes, the front view of the shoulders and body, and the side view of the legs. Draw a scene from your own classroom in the Egyptian style. Write a story about the scene. *(This student's drawing is of an Egyptian mummy. Notice all the hieroglyphics. This class studied hieroglyphics and then created compositions incorporating the symbols.)*

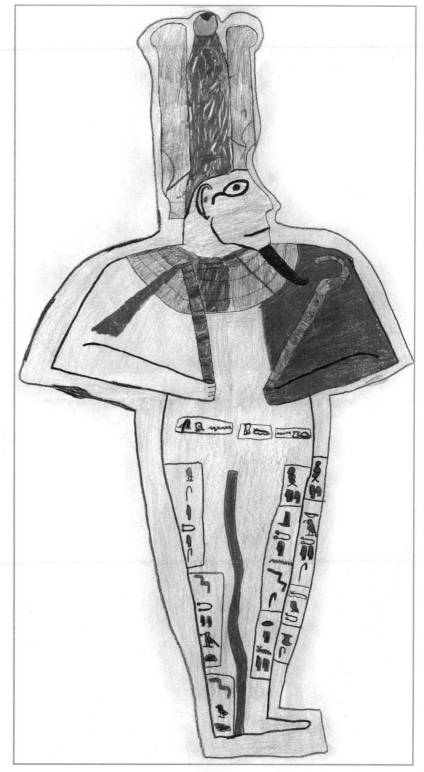

- Bring clothing to school that could be a costume or uniform for a person you are studying in social studies. Have your model wear the clothing and pose in a gesture that expresses that person. Do contour drawings of him or her. Write about that person's actions.

- Draw a future self-portrait. What would you like to be when you grow up? Draw yourself in the setting of your occupation. Write about your ambition.

- How do people dress in different parts of the world? Find videos or books about traditional dress in a variety of countries. Draw a model dressed in costumes for one country. Write about what you learned.

At the end of the school year, assign each chapter of your history textbook to a pair of students. Ask them to reread the chapter, find people and events that are important, and take turns posing as a person from the chapter while the other student draws.

- Write a brief summary of the event or person you drew, and make a booklet about the chapter. Here is an example. It is a drawing of Harriet Tubman, a former enslaved woman who courageously led others on the Underground Railroad to freedom.

- This drawing is an illustration of a scene from the play, *Prince Igor*. Notice the figure standing on a rug, and the horizon line (or floor line) that is drawn behind the figure. Draw an illustration of a scene from a story in your reading or social studies text. Think about dress and setting. Write a few sentences describing the scene.

19. Drawing Groups

This is an important concept. Gather photographs or magazine pictures and spend time looking at the way figures overlap. Note that as they go back in the picture, they seem smaller. The goals of these exercises are figure drawing, perspective through overlapping of forms and reduced size of objects in the distance, and composition.

*Teach **horizon line**—the line that separates the floor or ground from the background. Instruct students that when drawing people in a room, all of the feet should be below the horizon line.*

✏ Ask four classmates to pose in a group. All the students can stand or one student might sit with another student standing behind. Draw them as a group, drawing only what you see of the person behind. Suppose they are important officials and write a news story about an important meeting.

✏ Study Egyptian composition in wall paintings. Instead of showing foreground, background, and perspective, Ancient Egyptians divided the wall into geometric sections and told the story in sequence, as in a comic strip. All of the figures are drawn close up. There are no small figures in the distance. Using poses from your gym exercises, draw three stages of an exercise in the Egyptian composition form. Write an advertisement about the importance of exercise for health.

20. Cutting

Cutting Figures

Cutting is an excellent eye-hand-coordinating exercise. Give each student a 12" × 18" sheet of construction paper and a pair of scissors. Have a model pose facing the class. If necessary, ask students to move so that the entire class will have a frontal view of the pose. Side views are difficult to cut. Show students how to start cutting from the foot and cut up, holding the paper up in view of the model. Ask them to try to contain the entire figure in the 18" height. Encourage students to add details of feet and hands—no gingerbread cookies! Ask students to look at their completed figures to see if they have cut out both neck and shoulders, two parts of each arm, hands, and feet. Try to do this several times until all students seem to be catching on. Remind them of the importance of trying and learning from their mistakes. Consider making a bulletin board mural by arranging the figures together.

This kind of class project can be started in a drawing/writing period, and students can work on it over a period of weeks. Keep an overhead projector on hand so figures can be enlarged and traced. Details and background can be added with chalk, crayons, or tempera paint. Have students cut figures from poses related to an event in history. Use 6" × 9" sheets of construction paper so figures will be small enough to place on an overhead projector. Enlarge the figures on the overhead onto mural paper and plan a history mural.

✏ *(Give each student a 6" × 9" sheet of black construction paper and a 12" × 18" sheet of construction paper.)* Draw an action pose. Then cut a figure of an action pose from the smaller paper. Move the figure around on your large paper until you decide on an action to show. Then trace the figure many times into a strobelike action. Tracings may be drawn in transparency. This means that the entire figure is drawn each time. Glue the cut figure in the drawing when it is completed.

Cutting Letters and Inventing New Shapes

The cutting of shapes with scissors is a powerful learning device that develops eye-hand coordination. This skill provides many possibilities for learning in the classroom. For instance, cutting letters of the alphabet is a way of involving your students in every bulletin board in the room.

✏ *(Cut sheets of 12" × 18" construction paper into 4" × 18" strips. Give each student a strip and a pair of scissors.)* Cut a piece from your strip the width of the letter you want to cut. *M* and *W*, and round letters such as *O, G, Q,* and *D* will be wider than *A* or *E*. Look at the piece you have cut as a box that exactly contains that letter. Cut away the outside, keeping a straight edge like the line of a *B* or a *K*. Then cut away to make a thin or a thick letter. Pierce the center of a closed shape with the point of a pair of scissors and cut out the inside shape.

Start a bulletin-board word tile game with the cut letters. Put them in a box at the base of an empty bulletin board. Invite students to make words with the letters. If they need a letter that is not there, they can cut it! Pin or staple the words on the board and invite students to build on the words in a horizontal and vertical pattern.

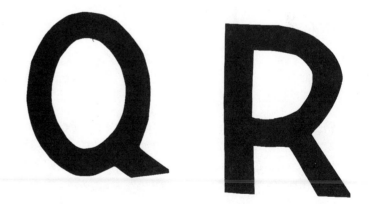

✏ Cut the letters of your name so that they "look like you"—tall, thin, funny, graceful, and so on. Glue them on a 12" × 18" sheet of construction paper and draw all of your favorite things around your name. *(This makes an excellent activity for the first day of school. Students learn how to cut letters, decorate the room, feel ownership, and you can learn their names.)*

Cutting Adjectives, Nouns, and Verbs

Begin an adjective board. Once students can visualize letters and cut them out, ask them to design the letters to look like the words they represent. Have each student cut one adjective and attach it to a bulletin board. Leave the display on the board and invite students to create more adjectives during free moments. Continue for a few weeks until the board is filled.

When the board is filled with adjectives, start a story on a long piece of mural paper folded into a large accordion-fold book. Invite students who have finished their work to use adjectives from the board to write a story in large letters with black markers. Each time they use an adjective, have them remove it from the board and glue it in the story. Continue developing the story until all the adjectives are used. You might create a verb board, a noun board, a participle board, and so on.

✏ Cut or draw the letters of these words to look like what the words mean.

WRITHING	RIGID	EXPLODING
HANGING	FALLING	FLYING
FLAMING	STORMY	FLUTTERING

✏ Find several different examples of how one letter appears in various magazines. Look for different styles and sizes. Cut them out carefully and glue them into a letter collage.

Have students cut the letters for your bulletin boards. They will pay much more attention to the displays.

Cutting Math Shapes

Teach positive/negative space. Give each student a 3-inch square of black construction paper. Ask students to cut a shape out of the square in such a way that the square is still there. Have them start at one side and return to the same side. Then mount all of the pieces in a checkerboard positive/negative pattern on a bulletin board.

✏ Start with a 4" square of black construction paper. Expand it by cutting a shape from the middle and flipping it up. Then, you might cut a smaller shape from that one and flip it down. Work on all four sides of the square, cutting from each side.

Glenita Ro

✏ *(Do a Math Multiples Metropolis. Give each student two 12" × 18" sheets of colored construction paper. They will need a ruler, a pencil, scissors, and glue. Assign a multiple, such as 10 which is a multiple of 5; or 9 which is a multiple of 3, to each student.)* Each of you will design a high-rise building in a modular pattern. This means rows of windows repeated on each floor. Your multiple is the pattern of the windows in your building. Decide how large your windows will be. If you have a large multiple, you will

have to be sure the windows will fit. If you want a tall building and you have 8" × 8", how can you make the building taller than it is wide? *(Elicit proportions of the windows: 1" wide and 2" tall. Insist on being careful when measuring, drawing lines, and cutting. When the window shapes are arranged, students may glue them in place.)* On a long piece of mural paper, arrange the buildings. Plan streets, cars, trees, and so on. Cut out figures, cars, and trees and glue them where they fit. Name your city and describe it.

21. Drawing Animals

Drawing animals, birds, fish, and insects helps students understand their structure and body parts. It also connects directly to your science curriculum. Build up a collection of photographs and make them available to your students to study carefully. Use encyclopedias, the Internet, National Geographic films, and so on, to observe both structure and movement of animals.

Encourage your students to draw animals in the same way they draw objects and figures—letting their eyes direct their hands. Have them use simple flowing lines that express shape and movement.

✏ Prehistoric artists drew on the walls of caves the animals they knew and hunted. This sketch was done while looking at the cave paintings in Lascaux cave in France. Notice how the outlines of animals overlap. Read about cave paintings and write about what you learn.

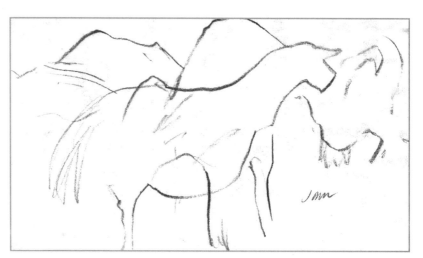

✏ This student drawing, in the style of the cave paintings, was done on brown kraft paper with a brush and black ink. When the drawing was complete, the student crumpled the paper and rubbed it with brown chalk to suggest the rough surface of the caves. Try this and write about your results.

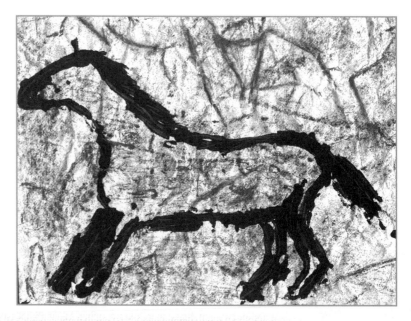

- Imagine a cat show. Draw a cat you think could win first prize. Write about it. Give it a name.

- This student drawing of a beaver uses many tiny lines to show its furry coat. Draw an animal with thick fur and show its texture.

- Find animals used in African totems and masks. The antelope was used by some Africans as a totem, or symbol, for speed in the hunt. Design an animal mask and write a story about its symbolism.

- Look at the photograph of this crocodile. Study the pattern of its skin. Draw your version of a crocodile, giving it an allover pattern.

- Draw yourself with your pet or with a pet you would like to have. Write a description of your pet and what you like about it.

22. Drawing Birds

✏ Study the shape and movement of birds from a film or a video. This line drawing was done quickly, while this row of birds alighted on a telephone wire. Look for pictures of birds on the Internet or in nature videos. Use a pencil or a fine-line marker and follow the graceful lines of the neck and the delicate tail feathers of birds. Write about these birds.

✏ This drawing of an owl was created by a sixth-grade student. Notice the many lines drawn to show feathers. Draw a bird and show its feathers in a layered pattern. What do you know about owls? Write your answers, or write some questions, in your journal.

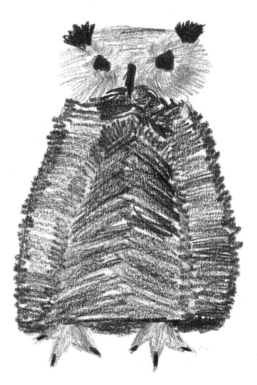

✏ Brilliantly colored tropical birds use their color as camouflage. Draw a tropical bird in a tree with brightly colored flowers. Try to hide the bird in the foliage of the tree.

✏ Look at books about ancient Egypt to find pictures of the ibis, a bird sacred to the Egyptians. This student drawing shows the ibis as an Egyptian god. Draw your version of the ibis and write about its role in Egypt.

23. Drawing Fish and Other Sea Creatures

You might correlate these drawing exercises with science lessons that discuss the structure and characteristics of fish and other sea creatures. Look for common body parts they share and the limitless variety in different kinds of sea creatures. Look for patterns and colors on the bodies of fish.

✏ In your science books or library reference books, find several species of fish. Study their shapes and patterns. Note all the body parts—fins, tail, gills, scales, and so on. Draw two or three in detail. Write about where your fish species lives—in fresh water or salt water, in coral reefs, and so on.

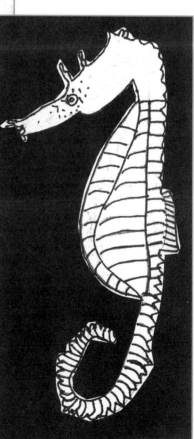

✏ Do you know what a sea horse looks like? It is a tiny creature with a head that really looks like the head of a horse. Find a photo of a sea horse. Draw your own. Then invent a sea rabbit or a sea giraffe and draw your version of one. Write a limerick about it.

✏ Draw a deep-sea environment. It might have seaweed, perhaps a coral reef, a school of small fish, starfish, jellyfish, or some large fish. What else could it have? Draw yourself as a deep-sea diver. Write about your deep-sea adventure.

✏ Draw a school of small fish swimming (a school of fish is a group of fish). They swim in a very rhythmic pattern. You might start your picture by drawing rhythmic curving lines lightly on your paper. Then draw many small fish along the line pattern. Write a haiku about them. *(See page 28 for the form of a haiku.)*

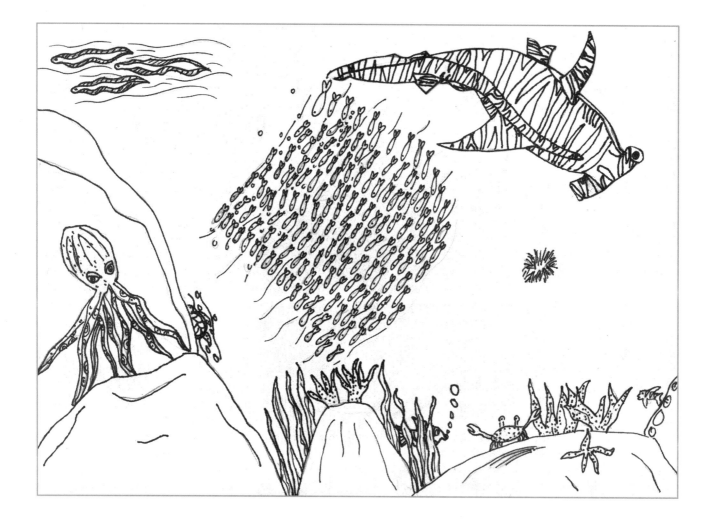

24. Drawing Insects

Study the structure of an insect's body, the symmetry, the number of legs, and its body parts—the head, antennae, thorax, abdomen, wings, leg parts. Find photographs of many species, or obtain a display from a museum.

✎ Draw a bee and its hexagonal honeycomb. Write a poem about how it flies to flowers to gather pollen.

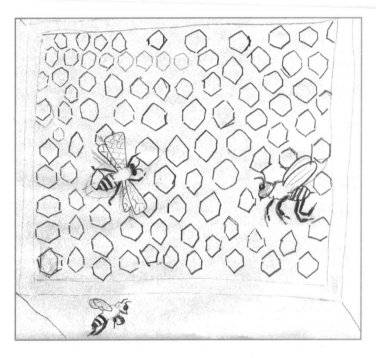

✎ Find pictures of insects. Note the number of legs and body segments each has. Look for color and pattern. Draw a picture of an insect you find or design one of your own. This is a student's drawing of a ladybug.

✏ Insects have protective coloration, or camouflage. Stick insects look just like little twigs. This drawing by a student shows them hiding on a branch. On the Internet or in a science book, find other insects that are camouflaged. Draw one and write about the predators from which it is hiding.

✏ Draw a centipede. *Centi* means "hundred." Does a centipede really have one hundred legs? Draw many segments of its body with a pair of legs for each segment. Write about walking with many legs.

✏ See how many insects you can hide in a drawing of a garden. Fill your paper with flowers, foliage, stems, and bugs. Write a poem about the garden. This is one student's drawing.

 How many legs does a spider have? *(eight)* Draw a spider in its symmetrical web.

This is one student's drawing.

25. Drawing Architecture

Buildings are so large that it seems daunting to try to draw them. For classroom reference, bring in several books on architecture from the library. Take your students outside with sketchbooks and pencils. Spend time looking at the school building or a house in the neighborhood. Ask students to note details—door, door frame, windows, roof lines, and so on. When students draw buildings, have them start with the door and work out from it, one detail at a time.

✏ Draw the front of your home or apartment building from memory. Think of the doorway, stairs, windows, and roof lines. When you get home, do another drawing of your home while you look at it. Compare the drawings. This is one student's drawing of her home.

Make a vocabulary list of structural forms—arch, lintel, column, capital, eaves, pediment, tower, spire, buttress, and so on.

✐ Draw pictures of each word on the vocabulary list. Write about a building you know that has some of these forms. These are student drawings of architectural forms. Can you identify the forms in each drawing?

Columns

✐ On graph paper, design a fast-food restaurant that serves healthy food. Use a tape measure to find out how much space a booth takes in your favorite restaurant. Use a scale of inches per foot. Plan the serving area, booths, doors, passageways, restrooms, and so on.

✐ Draw the façade, or the front, of your restaurant with a sign telling its name.

✐ Go outdoors on a fine day and draw the houses across from your school or draw the entrance to your school. Start with the door and just add each detail as you move out from the door. Write about the experience of drawing something this large.

✐ Design a house with solar heating panels on the roof. Describe how your system would work.

✐ Design a bridge for a river. Learn about suspension bridges, jackknife bridges, and so on. Write about what you learn.

✐ On large paper, draw the façade of a three-story building. Design the doorway and windows with pediments and other details. *(Attach all the class drawings to make a city mural, like this one.)*

26. Learning to Draw in Perspective

In Western art, perspective is a mathematical device used to show depth. An artist named Leon Battista Alberti devised perspective laws during the Renaissance. One-point perspective is based on a focal point at eye level on the horizon and parallel to the viewer's position. All horizontal lines are drawn at angles from that point. All vertical lines are drawn vertical. Teach perspective as an exercise in looking rather than a mathematical problem with a ruler.

Foreground and background are important in showing depth in a picture. In a landscape, the background will show a horizon line, or a line that separates the ground from the sky or the floor from the wall.

✏ Draw the hall outside your classroom. Draw the rectangle of the end wall small in the center of your paper. Hold your pencil up and, with one eye closed, point one end at the upper right corner of the far wall. Angle the pencil to follow the side wall. It will angle up. Do the same for the other side and for the floor lines. Find doors along the walls. They follow the same angle. But all the vertical lines will be straight down.

✏ When you draw in perspective, forms in the distance will be smaller. Trust your eyes to see this. Notice the smaller size of the buildings and the archway in this drawing of a street in Siena, Italy. Write about the problems you have in drawing in perspective. It is hard, but practice will help make it easy.

✏ A good way to see receding lines is to use a *finder*. In a 3" × 5" card, cut a 1" × 1 1/2" rectangle. Hold the finder to one eye and close the other eye. Frame off what you plan to draw. You will see the ceiling and floor lines as diagonals and the vertical lines will be straight.

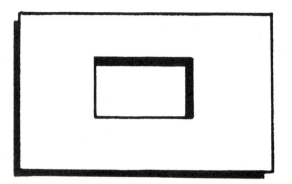

✏ Draw a scene in perspective and draw people in it. This student drawing shows a long banquet table and guests walking along it. Notice that the people in the foreground are drawn at the bottom of the paper.

Set up a chair on a desk or table. Have students draw it several times from different views. Place it in front of the room directly facing the students. Then turn it sideways, to the back, and finally on a diagonal. Looking up at the chair, students will be able to see the underside of the seat.

✏ Draw the chair from several views. Then write about how the shape changed as the chair was moved.

✏ Reducing the size in the background is another way to show depth in your drawing. This student drawing is an example.

✏ Another way to show depth in drawing is to overlap forms as they go back in space. This drawing shows the mesas and buttes of the Badlands in South Dakota. Draw your own scene of hills and mountains, overlapping as you build up in your picture. Tell about hiking in your hills.

27. Drawing Your Travels— Real or Wished For

✏ Study the architecture and natural forms of places you have learned about in geography. Research a place to which you would like to travel. Write requests for travel brochures to travel agencies or to tourist offices of foreign countries. Perhaps you can use the Internet to find out more about places of interest. This is a sketch of the town of Moltrasio on Lake Como in Italy. The town rises from the lake, and the houses seem to be on top of one another.

GRAND HOTEL IMPERIALE

moltrasio

✏ Look at a photograph of a special place you might like to visit. Find something in the photograph that you would like to draw. Look for the lines that make the shape of what you are drawing. Then add details as you see them. Read about this special place and write a description of it.

✏ This is a picture of a temple roof in Thailand. Look for similar roof shapes on buildings in many countries of Asia. Find out why these roofs curve up. Draw a picture of one and write about it.

✏ Design a poster advertising a place that you would like to travel to. Write about its special features.

✏ Find out about the shapes of traditional Native American homes in different parts of the United States. Some Native Americans lived in tepees. Others lived in longhouses. This is a photograph of Mesa Verde, in the southwest United States. These homes were built in eroding cliffs by Native Americans called the Anasazi. Research, then draw a picture of a traditional Native American home. Write about the materials needed to build it.

✏ This is a drawing of Artist's Point, a wonderful waterfall in Yellowstone National Park. Imagine a waterfall, and draw what it looks like. Write about discovering it.

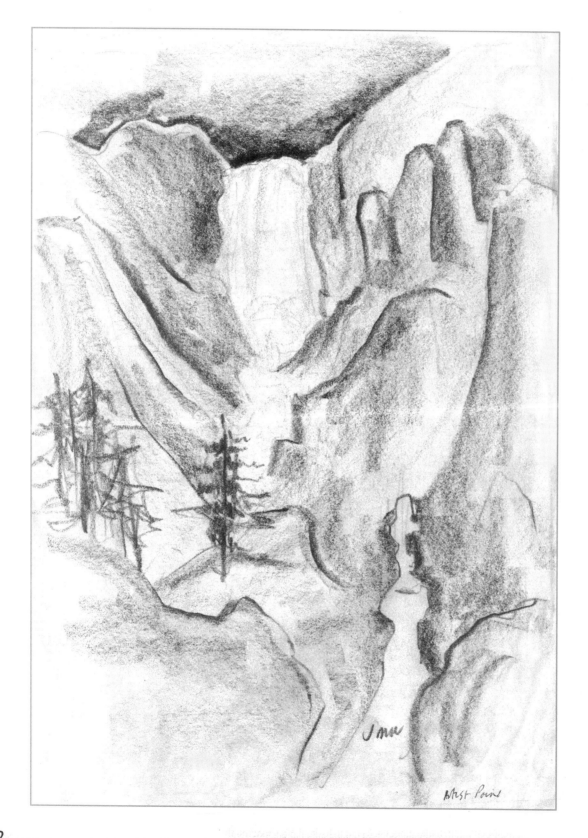

28. Drawing Maps

✐ City maps are designs for living. The first map is of Rome, Italy. It shows a pattern of irregular diagonals and curves. Rome is built on seven hills. The second map is of Florence, Italy. Compare the patterns in both maps. Florence is a flat area with a neat grid of streets. Florence was designed during the Renaissance. Obtain a map of a city you would like to visit. Write to the country's tourist office or find a map on the Internet. Study its street patterns—grid, radial pattern, and so on. Select a section of the city and draw the pattern of the streets. Write about why you chose that city.

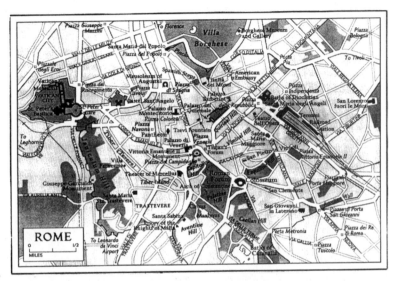

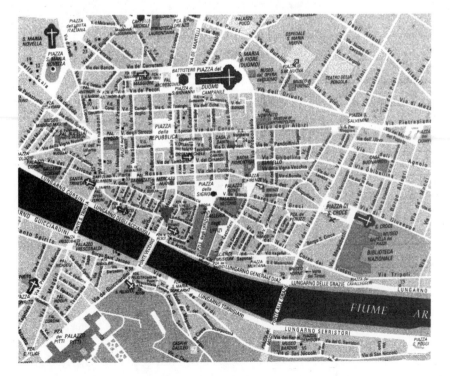

✏ Design your own city map. Will your streets be on a grid? Will they be circular? Some cities are designed with streets radiating from a center point. In Washington, D.C., the main streets radiate diagonally from the Capitol building. If a river runs through your city, the streets might follow its curve. Write about your city when you have finished designing it. This is a sixth-grade student's map. Enjoy its inventiveness.

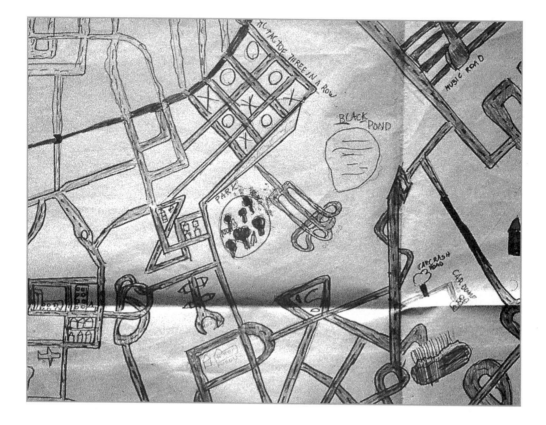

✏ Draw a map of your own neighborhood. Draw special buildings, parks, and shopping areas. Write an advertisement encouraging prospective homebuyers to look at your neighborhood.

✏ Design an ideal neighborhood. Plan blocks with homes, parks, a school, shops, museums, and so on. Write about your plan.

✏️ Draw a map of a place you would like to visit. This is a student's map of the Hawaiian Islands.

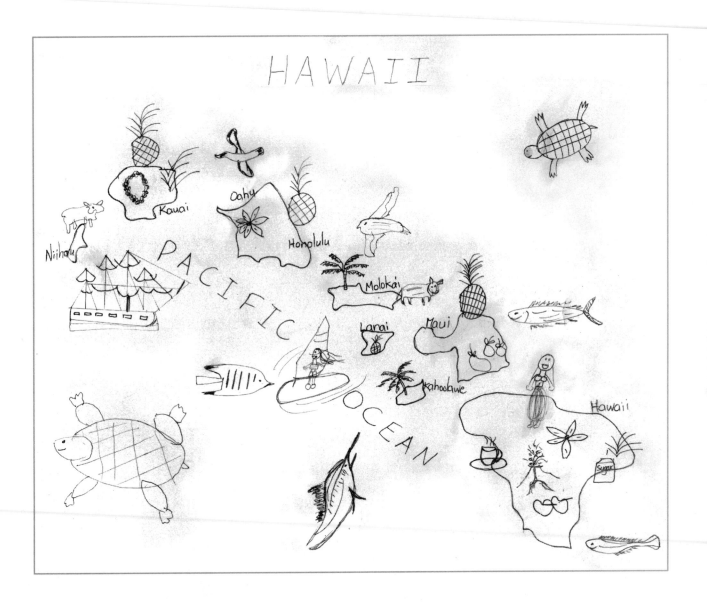

29. Drawing from Imagination

Imaginative thinking and expression are essential to learning. Students are then free to make new connections, to see relationships, and to come up with new ideas. The following activities are designed to stimulate this kind of thinking. Be open to your students' ideas. Encourage fantasizing, exaggerating, and combining both forms. If your students have ideas for drawing and writing exercises, listen to them and use their ideas.

✏ Devise a new kind of car or other new invention to help people. This is a student's idea of a car with a magnetic bumper that would push cars away before they crash. Draw your idea and write about it.

✏ Plan a cartoon strip. Work with a partner to think up the story and the characters. Then draw each character. Draw the actions in the order of how they will happen and then add dialogue in balloons. When the sketches are complete, use a large sheet of paper to redraw each part in sequence.

✏ Draw a figure from a posed model, and exaggerate the movement by enlarging or extending a body part. Can you draw a figure that looks jovial? Write about what has caused him or her to be jovial.

✏ Think of several idioms. Write them and draw what they would look like literally. For example: "I like to hang around." "She makes me sick." "I'm all tied up right now." "He burns me up." This is a student's drawing of "in a pickle."

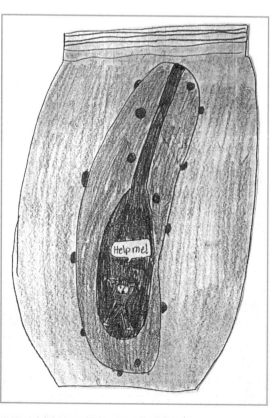

✏ *(Give an apple to each student along with an 18" × 24" sheet of drawing paper.)* First do a contour drawing of your apple in the upper-left corner of your paper. Now take one bite and draw the apple again, showing the shape of the bite. Continue taking bites, drawing the apple after each one, until you have just the core. Draw the core. Now go back to your drawings. Look at them and see what you can imagine in each one—a face? a continent? Add lines to each one to complete the new idea.

✏ Draw a "Wanted" poster. Invent your fugitive. Draw a front view and a profile. Then write a description and tell about his or her crime.

✏ Totems are symbols. An African antelope mask symbolizes the speed of the antelope. Think of images that are totems of people today—cars, computers, or even money. What else could be a present-day totem? Design a contemporary totem to tell about the values of today's society. This is a student's idea of designer jeans totem.

✏ This is a huge sculpture outside a temple in Thailand. It is a guardian figure. Its size makes it a "heroic" sculpture, but it is not as large as a "colossus" sculpture, such as the Statue of Liberty, which is many times human size. Draw your version of a guardian figure. Tell about what it is guarding.

✏ Artist Marc Chagall drew *Painter at His Easel*, below. What do you think he is saying about how he feels when he paints? Has he exaggerated the joy he gets from making art? Draw yourself doing something you enjoy. Can you exaggerate to show your feelings?

30. Encouraging Drawing at Home

The following pages offer many ideas for self-directed drawing at home. Allow students to take their sketchbooks home or suggest that they keep another sketchbook at home.

Encouraging students to draw at home has many advantages, starting with the possibility of weaning them away from television and computer games. Students who develop a habit of drawing not only will enjoy it, but they will build confidence that will last a lifetime. Give students credit for drawings done at home. Take time to look at them and, once in a while, display some "home" themes—my family, kitchen shapes, pets, and so on.

You may want to duplicate pages 91 through 93 and give them to your students to keep at home. Encourage them to add to the list ideas they have for drawing.

Drawing at Home

- Draw some kitchen gadgets—can openers, scissors, peelers, ladles, spatulas, whisks, and so on.

- Draw your desk and other furniture.

- Pile up some pots and pans, and draw the pile.

- Draw pieces of fruit and vegetables. Draw an orange. Then peel it halfway and draw it again. After you eat it, draw the peel.

- Draw your family members while they are working or while they are relaxing and watching TV. (You can get lots of drawing done during commercials.)

- Draw your closet. Follow the lines of each thing hanging in it, for example, rows of shoes.

- Draw your kitchen in perspective.

- Draw all the objects on your desk.

- Draw your room in perspective.

- Draw the cabinets in your kitchen.

- Arrange a blanket or another large piece of fabric in a heap. Draw its contours on your paper. When your drawing starts looking like hills, complete it as a landscape. Add trees, a road, and other forms.

- Draw your bicycle. On a sunny day, stand it in the sun. Place a large sheet of paper on the ground in its shadow and trace the shadow. (If you work too slowly, the shadow will change!)

✏ Draw your pet or pets. Do many views of each pet—lying down, standing, eating, or even moving.

✏ Draw the flowers in your garden or potted plants in your home.

✏ Draw the trees in your neighborhood.

✏ Lie on your stomach in the grass and look closely at the blades of grass, the dandelions, or other plants growing there. Do a drawing of every blade of grass. Each will have a different form. If you draw one blade at a time, it is not hard to complete a large area.

✏ Draw yourself in any environment you choose. Have a friend pose for you in the action you want. Complete the figure by adding the kind of clothes that you need in such an environment. Complete the background.

✏ Cut your shadow shape. Try standing in front of a bright light and play with your shadow on the opposite wall. Find a pose you like and cut your own shadow from a large sheet of paper. Experiment with the lamp. The closer to the lamp you stand, the larger your shadow will be. The closer you stand to the wall, the smaller your shadow will be. What will happen if the lamp is on the floor? How will you look if your shadow bends to the floor?

92

✐ Do a drawing right on the financial pages of a newspaper. Do a large drawing of a city skyline. Use a black marker.

✐ Keep a "visual log." Every day notice something about one place in your home. Write about it. After a week, draw that place. You will see it much better.

✐ Invite a friend over and pose for each other as characters from history. Find articles of clothing that could make costumes for the characters.

✐ Design the car of your dreams.

✐ Draw yourself as Superman or another superhuman character.

✐ Draw a portrait of yourself in a huge hat. Fill it with fruit, flowers, or kitchen utensils.

✐ Sit on the floor near your dining room table and draw what it looks like from there. Use the rules for perspective. Trust your eyes. See which way each line seems to go.

✐ Invent your own picture alphabet. Choose an image for each letter. First make a chart. Then write a story with your alphabet.

Glossary

action pose - a figure drawing which shows movement of the model

arch - a curved masonry construction for spanning an opening, consisting of wedge-shaped stones set to lean in and balanced with a keystone

asymmetrical balance - the balance achieved with shapes of different sizes

balance - a state of stability or equilibrium. In art it can be symmetrical or asymmetrical and achieved with color, shape, line, proportion, and so on.

bilateral symmetry - the same on both sides of a central axis

buttress - an external prop or a support added to steady a structure

camouflage - a disguise or deception, found in nature to protect animals

capital - the uppermost portion of a column, widened to support the roof

chiaroscuro - the distribution of light and shadow in a picture

column - a rigid, slender upright support for a building

complementary - completing; a necessary component

composition - the organization of parts to make a unified whole

concentric circles - circles of varying sizes drawn around one radial point

conical - having a cone shape

contour drawing - linear representation; all of the parts of a subject

crayon resist - the result of applying a wet wash of ink or watercolor over a solid crayon line or shape

cylindrical - having a tubular shape

diamante poem - a poem having seven lines and forming a diamond shape

dome - half of a sphere; an architectural roof form

eaves - the overhanging lower edge of a roof

ebony pencil - a soft lead pencil

flower parts - petal, sepal, pollen, stem, stamen, leaves, and pistil

gesture drawing - a quick line recording of the outer edge of a figure

grotesque - odd or unnatural in shape or appearance

horizon line - the line that forms the visual boundary between foreground and background

idiom - an expression having both literal and figurative meaning

keystone - a wedge-shaped stone set in the center of an arch to counterbalance the inward thrust

line quality - the thinness, thickness, smoothness, or irregularity of a line. Can be varied by tool or pressure.

lintel - a horizontal beam supporting the weight above an opening

metamorphosis - a complete change of form, structure or substance

modular - a design unit that is repeated

monasteries - houses for communities of religious men

mosaic - a design composed of many small pieces

overlapping - technique of showing depth; only the part seen is drawn

pediment - a low shape, usually triangular, above a horizontal structure, giving an angle to the roof

perceptual - pertaining to the senses, particularly sight

perspective - a drawing technique that represents volume and spatial relationships on a flat surface

positive/negative - figure and background, solid and open

proportion - the relation of parts to the whole in a composition

protective coloration - a coloration some animals assume to hide from predators

radial symmetry - symmetry that goes from the center outward

rhythm - the patterned repeat of an element (color, line, shape, and so on) in art

scratchboard - a design made by coating black ink over a crayoned surface and scratching through the ink

shape - a flat area enclosed by its boundary

simulated texture - giving the appearance of an actual texture

space - the designed surface of a picture; the illusion of depth in a 2-D plane

spire - a tall pointed pyramidal structure on a roof; steeple

still life - an arrangement of inanimate objects in a drawing or painting

tessellation - a shape that, when repeated, leaves no space between shapes. Example: floor tiles, which can be square, oblong, hexagonal.

texture - the visual (simulated) and/or tactile (actual) quality of a surface

three-dimensional - having height, width, and depth

topography - the relief features of a surface, such as the Earth

tower - a structure high and narrow

transparency - a technique of drawing that shows all the details of a form in the background

volume - cubic space or mas

Name _____

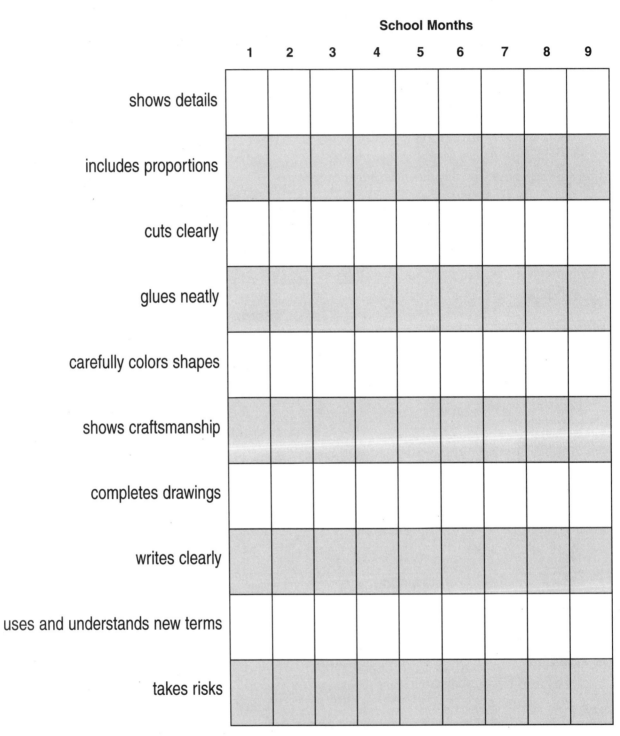

	School Months								
	1	2	3	4	5	6	7	8	9
shows details									
includes proportions									
cuts clearly									
glues neatly									
carefully colors shapes									
shows craftsmanship									
completes drawings									
writes clearly									
uses and understands new terms									
takes risks									